A Day with Baby

Di Taylor

Name _____

Age _____

Class _____

OXFORD
UNIVERSITY PRESS

UNIVERSITY PRESS

Great Clarendon Street, Oxford OX2 6DP

Oxford University Press is a department of the University of Oxford.
It furthers the University's objective of excellence in research, scholarship,
and education by publishing worldwide in

Oxford New York

Auckland Bangkok Buenos Aires Cape Town Chennai
Dar es Salaam Delhi Hong Kong Istanbul Karachi Kolkata
Kuala Lumpur Madrid Melbourne Mexico City Mumbai
Nairobi São Paulo Shanghai Taipei Tokyo Toronto

OXFORD and OXFORD ENGLISH are registered trade marks of
Oxford University Press in the UK and in certain other countries

ISBN 9780194400787

Printed in China

Illustrations by: Arlene Adams

With thanks to Sally Spray for her contribution to this series

Reading Dolphins
Notes for teachers & parents

📖 Using the book

1 Begin by looking at the first story page (page 2). Look at the picture and ask questions about it. Then read the story text under the picture with your students. **Use section 1 of the CD for this if possible.**

2 Teach and check the understanding of any new vocabulary. Note that some of the words are in the **Picture Dictionary** at the back of the book.

3 Now look at the activities on the right-hand page. Show the example to the students and instruct them to complete the activities. This may be done individually, in pairs, or as a class.

4 Do the same for the remaining pages of the book.

5 Retell the whole story more quickly, reinforcing the new vocabulary. **Sections 2 and 3 of the CD can help with this.**

6 **If possible, listen to the expanded story (section 4 of the CD). The students should follow in their books.**

7 When the book is finished, use the **Picture Dictionary** to check that students understand and remember new vocabulary. **Section 5 of the CD can help with this.**

💿 Using the CD

The CD contains five sections.

1 The story told slowly, with pauses. Use this during the first reading. It may also be used for "Listen and repeat" activities at any point.

2 The story told at normal speed. This should be used once the students have read the book for the first time.

3 The story chanted. Students may want to chant along with the story.

4 The expanded story. The story is told in a longer version. This will help the students understand English when it is spoken faster, as they will now know the story and the vocabulary.

5 Vocabulary. Each word in the **Picture Dictionary** is spoken and then used in a simple sentence.

Max is at home.
Baby Ben is at home, too.

1 Connect.

Max

Ben

Mom

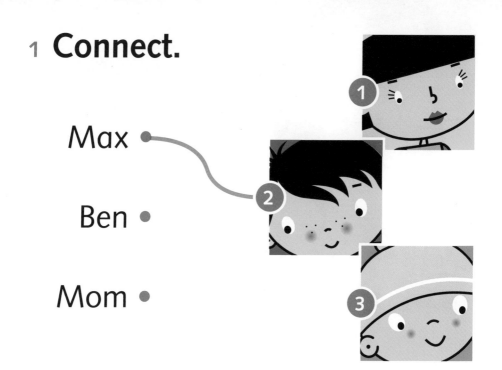

2 Circle yes or no.

1. Mom is at home.   **yes**   no
2. Max is at school.   yes   no
3. Max is at home.   yes   no
4. Ben is a baby.   yes   no
5. Max is a girl.   yes   no
6. Ben is happy.   yes   no

Max. Please play
with Ben.

Circle.

1 Max is ⟨helping⟩ / sleeping .

2 Ben is crying / happy .

3 Mom is working / playing .

4 Ben is big / little .

5 Max is holding a ball / baby .

6 Ben's hat is red / blue .

This is a book, Ben.
This is a dog.

Number.

boy [3]

book [ ]

baby [ ]

ball [ ]

cat [ ]

duck [ ]

Look, Ben.
This is a yellow duck.
This is a white cat.

Circle yes or no .

1. The duck is green.

    yes
    (no)

2. The duck is yellow.

    yes
    no

3. The cat is yellow.

    yes
    no

4. The hat is brown.

    yes
    no

5. The cat is white.

    yes
    no

6. The ball is blue.

    yes
    no

7. The monkey is brown.

    yes
    no

Here is a banana, Ben.
Here is some juice.

Connect.

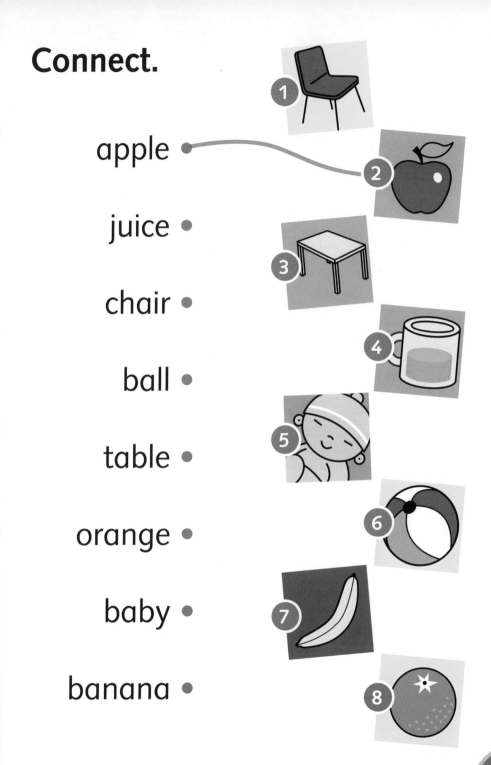

apple •

juice •

chair •

ball •

table •

orange •

baby •

banana •

11

Let's wash your face, Ben.
Let's wash your hands.

Circle.

❶ **Max** / **(Ben)** is a baby.

❷ **Max** / **Mom** is helping Ben.

❸ Ben is in the **kitchen** / **bathroom** .

❹ Ben has a **yellow** / **red** chair.

❺ **Ben** / **Max** has a clean face.

❻ Max has a blue **shirt** / **hat** .

Sleep well, Ben.
See you later.

1 **Circle** yes **or** no .

- ❶ Ben is crying.   yes (no)
- ❷ Max is in bed.   yes   no
- ❸ Max is happy.   yes   no
- ❹ Ben is happy.   yes   no

2 **Number.**

 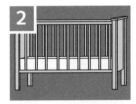 

boy   6   monkey ☐

bed ☐   cat ☐

baby ☐   duck ☐

Picture Dictionary

apple

bed

baby

blue

ball

cat

banana

chair

dog

juice

duck

monkey

face

orange

green

red

hand

yellow

Dolphin Readers

Dolphin Readers are available at five levels, from Starter to 4.

The Dolphins series covers four major themes:

Grammar, Living Together, The World Around Us, Science and Nature.

For each theme, there are two titles at every level.

Activity Books are available for all Dolphins.

All Dolphins are available on audio CD.
(2 TITLES ON EACH CD ⊙ SEE TABLE BELOW)

Teacher's Notes are available at **www.oup.com/elt/dolphins**

	Grammar	Living Together	The World Around Us	Science and Nature
Starter	• Silly Squirrel • Monkeying Around	• My Family • A Day with Baby	• Doctor, Doctor • Moving House	• A Game of Shapes • Baby Animals
Level 1	• Meet Molly • Where Is It?	• Little Helpers • Jack the Hero	• On Safari • Lost Kitten	• Number Magic • How's the Weather?
Level 2	• Double Trouble • Super Sam	• Candy for Breakfast • Lost!	• A Visit to the City • Matt's Mistake	• Numbers, Numbers Everywhere • Circles and Squares
Level 3	• Students in Space • What Did You Do Yesterday?	• New Girl in School • Uncle Jerry's Great Idea	• Just Like Mine • Wonderful Wild Animals	• Things That Fly • Let's Go to the Rainforest
Level 4	• The Tough Task • Yesterday, Today and Tomorrow	• We Won the Cup • Up and Down	• Where People Live • City Girl, Country Boy	• In the Ocean • Go, Gorillas, Go